W9-CHN-550

EARTH, SPACE, AND BEYOND

WHY IS THERE
LIFE ON EARTH?

Andrew Solway

Chicago, Illinois

www.heinemannraintree.com
Visit our website to find out
more information about
Heinemann-Raintree books.

To order:

☎ Phone 888-454-2279

💻 Visit www.heinemannraintree.com
to browse our catalog and order online.

© 2011 Raintree
an imprint of Capstone Global Library, LLC
Chicago, Illinois

Visit our website at
www.heinemannraintree.com

All rights reserved. No part of this publication may be
reproduced or transmitted in any form or by any means,
electronic or mechanical, including photocopying,
recording, taping, or any information storage and
retrieval system, without permission in writing from the
publisher.

Edited by Andrew Farrow, Adam Miller and Adrian
Vigliano
Designed by Marcus Bell
Original illustrations ©Capstone Global Library 2011
Illustrated by KJA-artists.com
Picture research by Hannah Taylor
Originated by Capstone Global Library Ltd.

Library of Congress Cataloging-in-Publication Data
Solway, Andrew.
   Why is there life on Earth? / Andrew Solway.
      p. cm.—(Earth, space, and beyond)
   Includes bibliographical references and index.
   ISBN 978-1-4109-4160-2 (hc)—ISBN 978-1-4109-4166-
4 (pb) 1. Life—Origin—Juvenile literature. 2. Earth—
Juvenile literature. 3. Life on other planets—Juvenile
literature. I. Title.
   QH325.S65 2012
   576.8'3—dc22   2010040160

Printed and bound in the USA.
009769RP

Acknowledgments
The author and publishers are grateful to the following
for permission to reproduce copyright material: Corbis
pp. 10 (©ESA/DLR/FU Berlin [G. Neukum]), 17 (©Reuters/
NASA), 18 (©Ralph White), 30 (©Charles O'Rear), 39
(©Chip Simons); NASA pp. 11 (JPL/ASI/ESA/Uni v. of
Rome/MOLA Science Team/USGS), 13 (DLR [German
Aerospace Center]), 15, 16 (JPL-Caltech),19, 20, 21, 27
(JPL), 28, 29 (JPL/USGS), 32, 33, 38 (JPL); Photolibrary
pp. 5 (©Pacific Stock/ Ed Robinson), 8 (©Imagebroker);
Science Photo Library pp. 7 (©Volker Steger), 12
(©British Antarctic Survey), 22 (©Tony & Daphne Hallas),
24 (©Chris Madeley), 25 (©NASA), 26 (©Animate4),
31 (©Dr M.Rohde,GBF), 34 (©A. Simon-Miller/GSFC/
NASA/ESA/STScI), 35 (©Detlev Van Ravenswaay), 36
(©European Southern Observatory), 37 (©Lynette Cook),
40 (©Philippe Psaila), 41 (©Jerry Lodriguss); shutterstock
p. 9 (©Janelle Lugge).

Cover photograph of Seedling Sprouting in Lava Field
reproduced with permission of Corbis (©Jon Hicks).

We would like to thank Professor George W. Fraser for his
invaluable help in the preparation of this book.

Every effort has been made to contact copyright holders
of any material reproduced in this book. Any omissions
will be rectified in subsequent printings if notice is given
to the publisher.

Disclaimer
All the Internet addresses (URLs) given in this book were
valid at the time of going to press. However, due to the
dynamic nature of the Internet, some addresses may
have changed, or sites may have changed or ceased to
exist since publication. While the author and publisher
regret any inconvenience this may cause readers, no
responsibility for any such changes can be accepted by
either the author or the publisher.

EARTH, SPACE, AND BEYOND

WHY IS THERE LIFE ON EARTH?

Contents

Some words are shown in bold, **like this**. You can find out what they mean by looking in the glossary. You can also look out for them in the "Word Station" box at the bottom of each page.

A Goldilocks Planet

In the story of Goldilocks and the three bears, Father Bear's porridge is too hot, Mother Bear's porridge is too cold, but Baby Bear's porridge is just right. The Earth is like Baby Bear's porridge — just right for life. It is sometimes called the "Goldilocks planet."

What makes Earth such a special place for life? For answers to this question, scientists have looked out into space to see how the Earth is different from its neighbors. Could there be life in the **solar system**, or beyond? To answer this question, many scientists are studying life at the extremes on Earth. They are learning that life can survive in a far broader range of conditions than had been previously thought.

Cooking up life

How did life begin? In 1953, some scientists thought that life began near the ocean surface. They put together some of life's ingredients from a mixture of simple chemicals that might have been in ancient oceans. However, discoveries since then have led to other theories. Life may have begun on the ocean bed, or in rocks. It may even have come from outer space.

However life began on Earth, one thing is certain. Without stars that shone and then exploded billions of years ago, there would be no life here at all. Our lives are linked to the solar system, the Sun, and the rest of the Universe.

Did we come from space?

Some scientists argue that simple life forms such as **bacteria** could have fallen to Earth in comets or asteroids, and provided the "seeds" for life on Earth. This theory is known as "panspermia."

Butterfly fish swim in a colorful shoal over a coral reef in Hawaii. The shallow, warm waters provide ideal conditions for life.

The Basics of Life: Water

Artificial life

A private research company in the United States has created what news reporters called "artificial life." In 2010 the J. Craig Venter Institute built a complete copy of the DNA (the genetic material) from a bacterium (one bacteria), using simple chemicals. They then replaced the DNA of another bacterium with the artificial DNA. The new bacterium is not exactly artificial life, but it is a step along the way. Dr. Craig Venter, the head of the company, said, "It's a living species now, part of our planet's inventory of life."

Living things can survive in the most unlikely places. But there is a bottom line. Life, at least as we know it, cannot survive without certain basic ingredients.

A precious liquid

The first essential is water. Some desert creatures can survive on the water they get in their food, while sea hunters such as killer whales and some sharks need huge areas of ocean to hunt in. But whether it is a droplet or an ocean, all living things need this precious liquid.

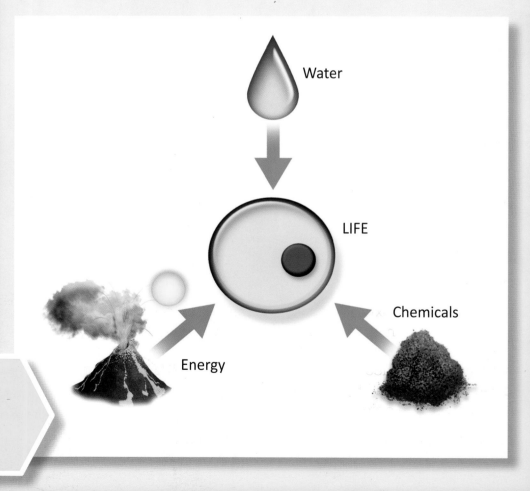

Water

LIFE

Chemicals

Energy

The essential ingredients for life are very simple: water, energy, and some basic chemicals.

Energy and chemicals

The second essential is energy. We need energy for obvious things such as running around or lifting heavy weights. But even if people stayed in bed all day, they would still need energy to keep their hearts beating and their lungs working. The natural tendency in the Universe is for things to decay and fall apart. But living things are highly organized, and keeping them that way requires energy.

Finally, life cannot exist without some basic chemicals. Living things are made mostly of four elements: carbon, hydrogen, oxygen, and nitrogen. These simple substances are built up into large, complex molecules such as **proteins** and **DNA**. Without these simple building blocks, especially carbon and oxygen, life cannot possibly begin.

Scientists looking for evidence of life beyond the Earth have concentrated on places that have these basic ingredients.

Dr. Craig Venter used high-powered computers like these to help unravel the secrets of human DNA. Now he is building new DNA molecules in an attempt to create artificial life.

The liquid of life

Water is one thing that living things cannot do without. Life probably began in the oceans, which cover over two-thirds of the Earth's surface. And water is the main substance in all animals and plants.

Why do we need water?

On the most basic level, life is about chemistry. All living things are made up of tiny building blocks known as **cells**. Each cell is a container full of chemicals. Every moment, there are hundreds of chemical reactions happening inside every living cell. But without water, most of these chemical reactions could not happen.

Bringing back life

Some plants, fungi, and bacteria survive very harsh conditions in special structures called seeds, **spores**, or **cysts**. All of these have a tough, thick outer layer that protects a tiny spark of life inside, ready to burst out when conditions improve.

Scientists in Israel managed to grow an extinct kind of date palm from seeds that had been **dormant** for over 2,000 years. Bacteria may be able to survive even longer. In the year 2000 a team of scientists found bacteria that they think are over 250 million years old. They got the bacteria to grow again by providing water and food. However, other scientists disagree with these findings.

Welwitschia plants can survive for up to 2,000 years in the hot, dry Namib Desert. They get all the water they need from the fog that covers the desert early each morning.

There are many desert areas in the world, where there is little or no water. Yet even in these places, animals and plants do manage to survive. How can they do this?

The answer is that in most deserts, there *is* water, but only a little. Many animals and plants have an outer layer that stops water from escaping. This helps to conserve what water they have. Plants such as cacti (more than one cactus) store water in their stems or leaves. In hot deserts, many smaller animals save water by staying underground during the day.

But if there is no water at all, even the best-adapted organisms cannot survive. In some parts of the Atacama Desert in Chile, rain has never been recorded. These areas truly are lifeless. Not even bacteria or other microbes have been found there.

The spikes that cover a thorny devil offer more than protection. Drops of rain or dew run along tiny channels in the animal's thorny skin and then into its mouth.

"The Atacama is the only place on Earth [where] I've taken soil samples to grow microorganisms back at the lab and nothing whatsoever grew."

Fred A. Rainey, U.S. microbiologist

cell basic unit of living things: a capsule of living material surrounded by a thin outer membrane

Water in space

Earth is the only planet in the solar system with liquid water on its surface. But is there anywhere else in the solar system where life could possibly survive?

Today, Mars is a cold, dry planet, but in the past the planet had plenty of surface water. The evidence for this is carved into the rocks. Pictures of the surface of Mars show huge canyons and valleys, far larger than those that we have on Earth. These features must have been made by water.

There are many theories about how the huge valleys on Mars were formed. But detailed photos sent back from the space probe Mars Global Surveyor have led scientists to think that many of the huge canyons were formed by "flash" floods.

A view of the Martian surface from the Mars Express space probe. The features on the surface were produced by massive floods that happened millions of years ago.

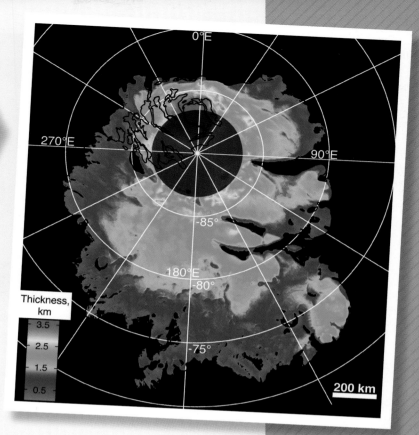

A map of the South Pole of Mars showing the thickness of ice there. There is enough water in the Martian ice cap to cover the whole planet to a depth of 11 meters (36 feet).

Thickness, km

Formed in a flash

In a flash flood, huge amounts of water are suddenly released in a great gush. The water flows downhill, carving through rocks as it travels.

On Earth, large flash floods can happen if a dam holding a lake of water in place is eroded away. The water in the lake suddenly breaks out of the dam and causes a flash flood.

On Mars, something similar may have happened, but on a massive scale. One canyon that scientists have studied is over 2,000 meters (nearly 7,000 feet) deep, and 885 kilometers (550 miles) long. The flood that produced it came from a lake which contained five times more water than all of the Great Lakes put together.

The surface water on Mars disappeared millions of years ago. So where did it go? Some water was lost into space. But in 2008 the robotic spacecraft Phoenix landed on Mars near the north pole and scooped up soil samples. The samples were found to be full of small lumps of ice.

Life on Mars!

News reports are not always reliable. In 2010 the front-page news was that NASA scientists had found "compelling new evidence of life on Mars." The reports seemed to say that fossils of "pond scum" had been found on Mars in a soft kind of rock called gypsum. In fact, scientists had found microscopic fossils in gypsum on Earth. The scientific report simply suggested that if there was life on Mars in the past, there might be fossil evidence of that life in the gypsum deposits there.

Simple insects like this springtail are among the few living creatures that can survive Antarctic conditions.

Life in ice

Under the Vatnajökull Glacier in Iceland there are many ice caves. Scientists have found bacteria living deep within the ice. The bacteria produce a kind of antifreeze that enables them to melt a tiny pocket of liquid water to live in. It would be possible for bacteria like this to live in the ice on a moon such as Europa.

Water in the frozen zone

Today, the surface of Mars is too cold for liquid water. The average temperature is –63°C (-81.4°F), colder than Antarctica in winter. But further out from the Sun, where it is even colder, space probes have found evidence of liquid water. Jupiter and Saturn are the two biggest planets in the solar system, and they have the most moons. This far from the Sun, it should be far too cold for water to be liquid. The planets themselves show no evidence of liquid water. However, some of the moons are more interesting.

The smoothest moon

Europa is the second of Jupiter's four large moons, between Io (the closest) and Ganymede. It is about the size of Earth's moon, and most of it is rock. But over the rocky core there is a thick layer of ice.

The icy surface of Europa is extremely smooth: it has the smoothest surface of any planet or moon. Over most of its surface there are no craters from meteors hitting the surface. However, the surface is criss-crossed with many grooves about 25 kilometers (15.5 miles) across.

Scientists think that the surface of Europa is smooth because below the icy surface there is a planet-wide ocean of liquid water. The grooves on the surface are where the ice has cracked and water has come up from below to fill the cracks.

Warmed by the tides

How can there be liquid water in such a cold region? The answer seems to be **gravity**. As Europa orbits Jupiter, different parts of the surface are pulled by Jupiter's gravity. This is like the daily tides we get on the Earth due to the pull of the Moon.

Jupiter's tidal pull on Europa is much greater than the Moon's tidal pull on Earth, because Jupiter's gravity is about 15 times greater than the Moon's. Europa is also affected by Io and Ganymede, which have smaller tidal pulls. The constant stresses as Europa's surface is pulled one way and then another generate heat energy. The heat produced is enough to keep the water below Europa's surface liquid.

Moons with antifreeze

Saturn's moons Titan and Enceladus also have liquid water below the surface. On these moons it is not the tides that keep the water liquid. Scientists have found evidence that there is ammonia mixed with the water. The ammonia acts as an antifreeze, which keeps the water liquid even at very low temperatures.

The cracked surface of Europa is broken up into massive blocks. Scientists think the surface is ice, with a liquid ocean beneath.

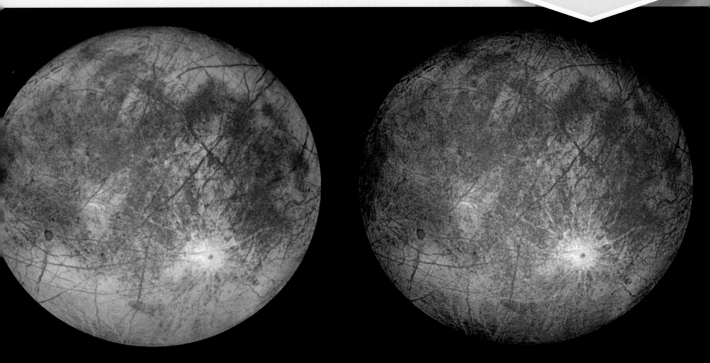

The Basics of Life: Energy

Many of the most important chemicals in living things are complex, delicate substances that are hard to make and easily destroyed. Making these subtances, and keeping them working, needs a constant input of energy. Without energy, living things quickly die.

The ultimate source

On Earth the main energy source is the Sun. It is a golden powerhouse that pours down light and heat every second of the day. A web of energy connects the Sun to all living things.

How does this work? Well, all animals get their energy from food, which is either other animals, or plants. Originally, all animal food comes from plants, because animals either eat plants directly, or eat animals that themselves eat plants.

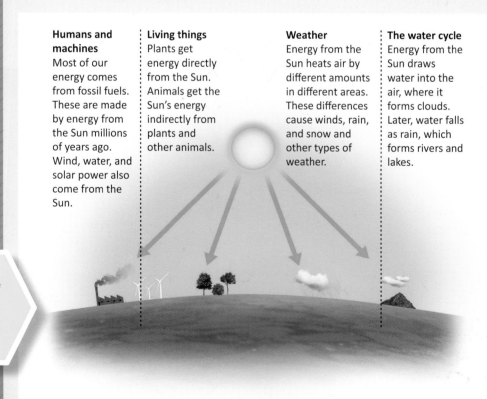

Humans and machines
Most of our energy comes from fossil fuels. These are made by energy from the Sun millions of years ago. Wind, water, and solar power also come from the Sun.

Living things
Plants get energy directly from the Sun. Animals get the Sun's energy indirectly from plants and other animals.

Weather
Energy from the Sun heats air by different amounts in different areas. These differences cause winds, rain, and snow and other types of weather.

The water cycle
Energy from the Sun draws water into the air, where it forms clouds. Later, water falls as rain, which forms rivers and lakes.

The Sun provides the energy for almost everything that happens on Earth.

The Sun produces energy by a process called nuclear fusion. In fusion, hydrogen atoms are squeezed and heated until they fuse (join) to make helium, which releases huge amounts of energy.

Fossil power

Have a look around your home: where does the energy you use come from? Most devices that need energy, from washing machines to watches, use electricity. And most of our electricity is made in power stations using **fossil fuels** — oil, coal, or gas. All these fuels are made from the remains of living things from millions of years ago. Ultimately all this energy comes from Sun power. Other kinds of energy we use, such as solar power, wind energy, and hydroelectricity, also come directly or indirectly from the Sun. The only energy we use that does not depend on the Sun is nuclear power.

Energy connections

Plants make their own food (energy) by a process called **photosynthesis**. They use energy from the Sun to combine carbon dioxide from the air with water from the soil to make sugars. Animals get their energy from plants, which make their energy from the Sun.

When animals and plants die, the complex chemicals that took so much energy to make are not wasted. They go to feed decomposers such as worms, fungi, and bacteria. Decomposers break down the chemicals of life into very simple substances called **minerals**. Minerals enrich the soil, providing the nutrients that plants need to grow properly.

Thick clouds full of sulfuric acid swirling across Venus make it impossible to see the surface.

CASE STUDY:

Climate change on Venus

In the past, Venus was affected by runaway climate change. Today we are seeing climate change on Earth, caused mainly by carbon dioxide produced when we burn fossil fuels. In 2007, a team of scientists studying the seasons on Mars found that the climate there is also warming rapidly. The scientists think that the cause is huge dust storms, which work like greenhouse gases and trap heat near the surface.

Third planet from the Sun

Earth is the third planet from the Sun. Mercury and Venus are too hot, Mars is too cold — but Earth is just right. The temperature on much of the Earth is just right for water to remain a liquid.

To understand why Earth's temperature is just right, let's look at our nearest neighbors in space.

Venus

At one time Venus, like Mars, may have had large oceans. But because Venus is hotter than Earth, more of the water evaporated into the **atmosphere** and became water **vapor**.

Water vapor is a powerful greenhouse gas. It stops some of the Sun's heat from escaping into space. As water vapor built up in the atmosphere, the planet got hotter and hotter. Eventually it got so hot that the water vapor itself split apart, into hydrogen and oxygen. The hydrogen was so light that it escaped into space, while the oxygen combined with sulfur hurled out by erupting volcanoes. This formed the huge clouds of choking sulfur dioxide that cover the surface of Venus today.

Sulfur dioxide is also a greenhouse gas, so Venus is now the hottest planet in the solar system. Surface temperatures can reach 484°C (903.2°F) — hot enough to melt lead.

Mars

Mars is smaller than Earth, and further from the Sun. Venus is too hot for liquid water to survive, while Mars is too cold. Winters are twice as long as on Earth, and winter temperatures fall to almost −125°C (−193°F). On summer days the temperature in some areas can reach 20°C (68°F). This is warmer than some places on Earth. However, if small amounts of ice do melt and form water, it quickly evaporates.

A dust storm erupts on Mars. In the left-hand picture, the storm is a small oval at the bottom right. In the second picture, the storm has spread across the whole planet.

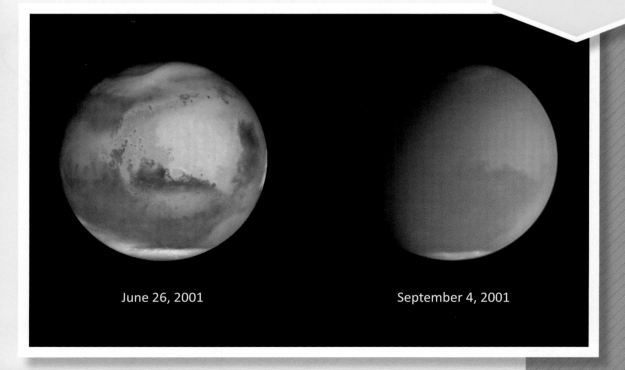

June 26, 2001

September 4, 2001

Other energy sources

In 1976, a scientific survey ship was mapping the ocean floor near the Galapagos Islands in the Pacific. The ship picked up evidence of hot water deep below the surface. The water was coming from the first **hydrothermal vent** to be discovered. Hydrothermal vents are hot springs under the ocean, where water as hot as 360°C (680°F) gushes up from the ocean floor.

In 1977, a special deep-water submarine (known as a submersible) went down to investigate these hydrothermal vents. Scientists were astonished to find that the areas around each vent were swarming with life. There were clams as big as loaves of bread, tube worms as tall as sunflowers, and crowds of white crabs. But the most important creatures at these vents are microscopic. They are bacteria that get energy and make food from the hot, chemical-rich water gushing from the vents. Because of these bacteria, a whole hydrothermal vent community can survive without the Sun's energy.

Sea life such as tube worms and tiny crabs are able to live next to this hydrothermal vent on the ocean floor.

In 2006, a front wheel on the Mars rover Spirit stopped working. Later, the broken wheel scraped off an area of surface soil and uncovered a patch of ground rich in silica.

Geysers on Mars

In 2008, some news reports said that geysers like those in Yellowstone National Park may once have bubbled up on Mars. The stories were based on the discovery of rocks rich in **silica** by the Mars rover vehicle Spirit. On Earth, rocks rich in silica are only found around hot springs and geysers.

Choking caves, roasting rocks, and snottites!

Living things around hydrothermal vents are not the only creatures that survive without the help of the Sun. In caves full of the rotten egg smell of hydrogen sulfide, scientists have found strange bacteria called snottites. These hang from the cave roof like strings of white, sticky goo. Snottites also use sulfur chemicals to make energy and food.

Even more incredible are bacteria living in rocks over 6 kilometers (almost 4 miles) below ground. The rocks at this level are hot, and the bacteria survive using this heat energy, plus chemicals dissolved in water that trickles through the rocks.

All these discoveries suggest that there are many other places in the solar system where life could survive. On rocky planets, life could survive in caves, or deep in the rocks if the surface environment is too harsh. They would not need sunlight to survive, only a source of heat and a few chemicals.

The Atmosphere

In parts of Russia, the average temperature can range from –25°C (–13°F) in winter to 16°C (61°F) in summer. This is a temperature range of 41°C (106°F) – the largest on Earth.

On the Moon, the average temperature changes from 107°C (225°F) to –153°C (–243°F) within *one day*. And yet the Moon is the same distance from the Sun as the Earth. Why is there such a huge difference?

This photo shows the thin blue layer of air that protects Earth from too much heat or cold.

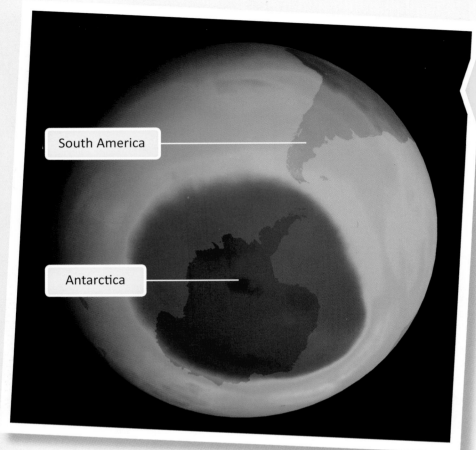

South America

Antarctica

Every year between August and December, an ozone hole forms over Antarctica. The area under this hole has virtually no protection from ultraviolet radiation.

A blanket and sunscreen

The Moon has much bigger temperature changes than the Earth because it has an atmosphere that **insulates** poorly. Air is a very good insulator. It keeps Earth warm, and stops us from roasting by day and freezing at night. Without the atmosphere, living things would not survive here.

The gases in the air are also vital to life. Animals and plants depend on oxygen from the air to help turn their food into useful energy. And during the day, plants use carbon dioxide from the atmosphere for photosynthesis. Without carbon dioxide, they would not be able to make food.

The atmosphere is also the ultimate sunscreen. When people go out unprotected in strong sunlight, they can easily get sunburned. This is because sunlight contains harmful rays such as ultraviolet radiation, which cause cancer and other kinds of sickness. The atmosphere blocks most of these harmful rays. Without it our skin would burn to a crisp in minutes.

Aerosol spray

High in the atmosphere there is a layer of air that is rich in a special type of oxygen known as ozone. At ground level ozone is harmful and causes smog. But the high-level ozone layer absorbs much of the ultraviolet radiation from the Sun. In the 1970s scientists discovered that chemicals released into the air by aerosol sprays cause damage to the ozone layer. The worst-affected areas are over Antarctica. Since then, scientists and governments have urged people to replace aerosol spray products with less-harmful products.

One final protection the atmosphere provides is from space invaders. As the Earth orbits the Sun, it is bombarded with small pieces of rock known as meteoroids. Each year, thousands of meteoroids burn up as they fall through the atmosphere. At night we see the fiery trails they leave as meteors, which are also known as shooting stars.

How Earth's atmosphere evolved

Today's atmosphere is mostly oxygen and nitrogen. But the atmosphere on the early Earth was very different. It was a mix of carbon dioxide, water vapor, ammonia, and sulfur compounds that would be poisonous to most living things today. The first living things evolved to live in this poisonous atmosphere. They were probably bacteria-like creatures that fed on nutrients dissolved in the water. They did not breathe oxygen, because there was none available at the time.

About 3½ billion years ago, new kinds of bacteria called cyanobacteria evolved. These bacteria were like plants — they could make their own food by photosynthesis. In the photosynthesis process, oxygen is produced as a waste product. The cyanobacteria started a process that gradually changed Earth's atmosphere. Over millions of years, cyanobacteria — and later other plant-like creatures — released oxygen as a waste product. Gradually, oxygen levels in the atmosphere rose.

The build-up of oxygen in the atmosphere led to new living things that could use the oxygen to release energy from their food. More plant-like creatures also evolved, and the levels of oxygen in the atmosphere kept rising. Around 700 million years ago, oxygen in the atmosphere reached the levels we see today.

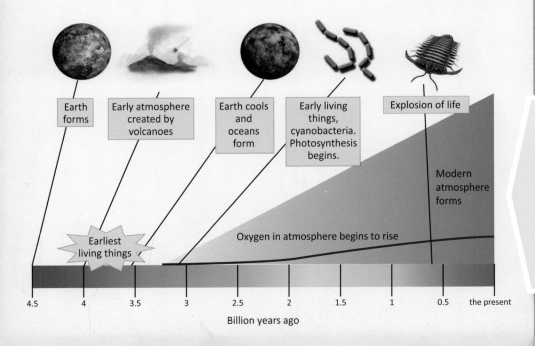

Earth forms

Early atmosphere created by volcanoes

Earth cools and oceans form

Early living things, cyanobacteria. Photosynthesis begins.

Explosion of life

Modern atmosphere forms

Earliest living things

Oxygen in atmosphere begins to rise

The atmosphere has changed significantly since the Earth began. The earliest living things arose in an atmosphere that would be poisonous to living things today.

| 4.5 | 4 | 3.5 | 3 | 2.5 | 2 | 1.5 | 1 | 0.5 | the present |

Billion years ago

The solar wind

The Sun does not just pour out energy. It also constantly produces a stream of microscopic, electrically charged particles known as the **solar wind**.

The solar wind blows across the solar system, bombarding everything in its path. It is strong enough to gradually strip away the atmosphere of a planet. However, the Earth does have some protection. It is surrounded by a magnetic field, as if it had a giant bar magnet right in the center. The magnetic field is caused by movements of **molten** iron within the Earth's core. It extends thousands of kilometers out into space, forming an invisible force field called the **magnetosphere**.

Where the solar wind meets the magnetosphere, most of the charged particles are deflected around the Earth rather than colliding with the Earth's atmosphere.

When solar wind particles collide with the magnetosphere, a colorful display of lights called an aurora can be seen from some places on Earth's surface.

This image shows Saturn's moon Titan, one of the rare examples of a moon that has its own atmosphere (see below for more on Titan's atmosphere).

Venus and Mars do not have magnetospheres like Earth. On Venus the thick carbon dioxide atmosphere is heavy and the pull of Venus's gravity prevents it from being easily stripped away. However, Mars is smaller than Earth and Venus, and so has less gravitational attraction. The combination of a lower gravity and the solar wind has removed most of Mars's atmosphere.

Other atmospheres

The Earth is kept warm and protected by its atmosphere. But why does the Earth *have* a protective atmosphere, while our closest neighbor, the Moon, does not? The answers are all about size.

Every object is attracted to other objects by the force of gravity. The more **mass** an object has, the stronger its gravity is.

When the planets were first formed, they had atmospheres rich in hydrogen. However, hydrogen is very light, and none of the rocky inner planets (Mercury, Venus, Earth, and Mars) had enough gravity to keep a hydrogen atmosphere. Mercury is so small that it has barely been able to hold on to any kind of atmosphere at all. Each of the larger three planets have atmospheres of some kind.

Titan's atmosphere

Moons should be too small to hang on to an atmosphere. But Saturn's moon Titan has an atmosphere that is thicker than Earth's and extends much further out into space. It is also similar to Earth's — it is mostly nitrogen. Scientists do not fully understand how Titan's atmosphere developed. The most likely theory is that the gases that make up the atmosphere came from volcanic activity in the past.

The right chemicals

Living cells, the basic units of life, are tiny chemical factories. Some cells can make the complex chemicals of life from the simplest ingredients. To do this, they need to have the right chemical ingredients. Without these ingredients life cannot develop.

Organic chemicals

The chemicals of life are all based on the **element** carbon. Carbon is so closely associated with life that chemicals made from carbon are called organic compounds (organic means connected with life). Carbon atoms can combine in a huge variety of ways. No other element can make such a vast array of different substances.

In addition to carbon, living things need several other elements — hydrogen, oxygen, and small amounts of other elements, such as calcium and iron. So, when scientists are looking at places beyond Earth where life could possibly exist, they check that the right chemicals are available.

Organic molecules can be really huge. This model shows just a small section of a molecule of DNA, the genetic material. A DNA molecule can contain billions of atoms, connected together in two long, spiraled chains.

Getting more complex

It is not enough simply to have the right elements to make life. Elements are the simplest of substances, but the chemicals of life are very complex. Conditions have to be right for more complex chemicals to develop. Water and energy are important for this. Many chemicals dissolve in water — once they are dissolved it is easier for them to join up and react together. Energy is important because many chemical reactions need a shot of energy to get them going. So a warm, watery chemical soup should provide the best conditions for life to develop.

Kick-starting life

The earliest life appeared on Earth about 200 million years after the planet cooled. Scientists believe that it should have taken much longer than this for complex chemicals to form. One explanation suggested is that Earth could have received chemicals from space. The huge clouds of gas that act as star nurseries have a rich mix of elements in them. Over perhaps a billion years, complex chemicals could develop in these clouds. Some scientists think that comets and asteroids landing on the early Earth could have brought chemicals such as amino acids to Earth from distant gas clouds, and given life a kick start.

The space probe Stardust picked up samples of dust from the comet Wild 2 and sent them back to Earth. The dust was found to contain many different organic compounds.

Signs of Life

Earth is not the only planet in the solar system with the basic chemistry set needed for life. Other moons and planets have the four most important elements (carbon, hydrogen, oxygen, and nitrogen). A few places in the solar system have organic compounds such as **methane**.

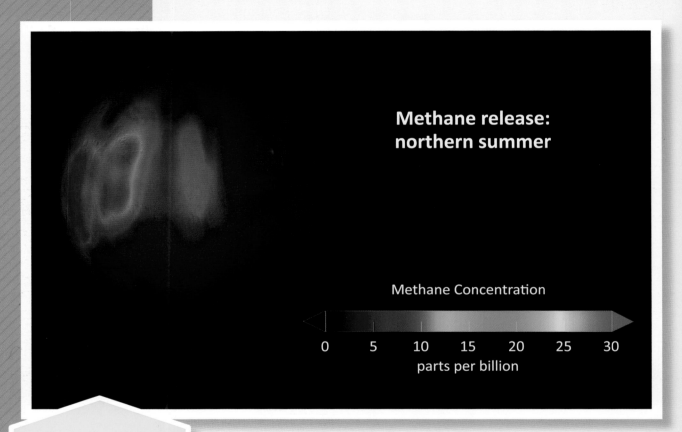

Methane release: northern summer

Methane Concentration

0   5   10   15   20   25   30
parts per billion

In the northern summer on Mars, high concentrations of methane build up in one area. This shows that methane is being released from an active source on the planet.

Plumes on Mars

One of the most exciting discoveries in recent years is the existence of methane in the Martian atmosphere. On the surface of Mars, methane is quickly broken down by the sunlight. So the methane in the atmosphere is being renewed regularly. Scientists have found that the methane is coming out of the ground, from hotspots in the northern hemisphere. The methane is produced only during the northern summer.

On Earth, the biggest source of methane is living things. It is produced by tiny microbes called methanogens. So it is possible that the methane on Mars is produced by microbes living underground.

Another possibility is that the methane is produced by volcanic activity in the rocks. Scientists currently think that Mars is geologically dead, meaning the core of Mars is solid rather than molten. If the methane is produced by volcanic activity, scientists will be proved wrong.

Organic rain

Another place that is rich in organic chemicals is Saturn's moon Titan. At the surface, the atmosphere of Titan contains about five percent methane, plus small amounts of other organic compounds. The surface of Titan is very cold — so cold that methane and other gases sometimes condense and fall from the sky as rain. On the surface of Titan there may be rivers and streams, lakes and ponds full of liquid methane, rather than water. Some scientists have suggested that there could be a whole different kind of life on Titan, based on methane rather than water.

The science of farts!

Methanogens on Earth live in oxygen-free conditions and "breathe out" methane as a waste product. Methanogens are found in wetlands and in seabeds, but also in the guts of humans and other animals. They are responsible for flatulence (the release of gases from the gut, or farts). Cows give out so much methane from their guts that the methane they produce is contributing to the greenhouse effect.

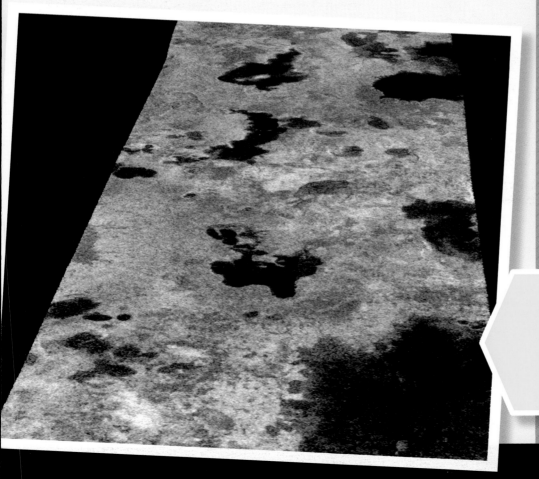

A radar picture of the surface of Titan taken by the space probe Cassini. The dark blue patches seen here are lakes of liquid methane.

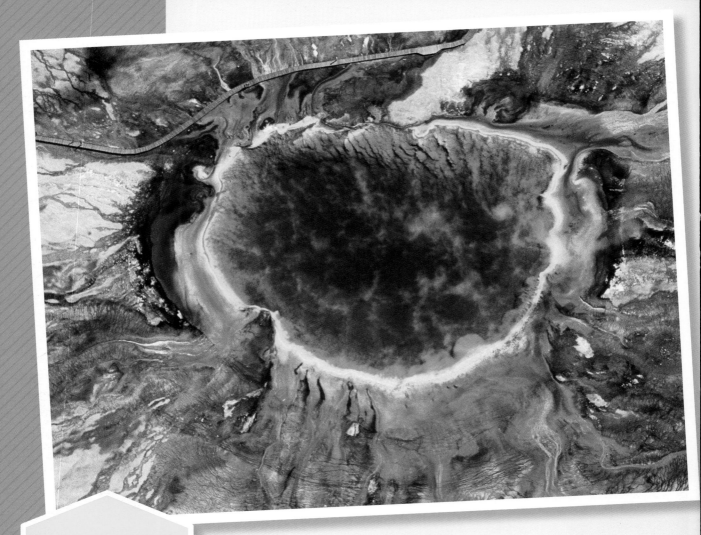

A true color image of the grand prismatic spring in Yellowstone National Park. The colors around the edge of the spring are produced by several kinds of archaea.

Aliens on Earth

There are endless stories and movies in which aliens invade the Earth. In the stories these strange life forms often arrive in flying saucers and try to destroy the human race. In recent years, scientists have found strange life forms on Earth. They have been here for billions of years, and some of them have proved to be useful to humans.

We have already learned about living things found in deep caves, in ice, in rocks, and in hydrothermal vents. The living things found in these places are unusual microbes that are found in extreme environments all over the Earth. They look like bacteria, but in some ways these microbes differ from all other living things. They are so unusual that scientists have decided they must form a completely new kingdom – the Archaea.

Different kinds of archaea are divided into four broad groups, depending on what conditions they live in. Halophiles live in extremely salty conditions. For example, Owens Lake in California is an almost dry salt lake with a thick, crust of solid salt at the surface. Halophiles grow on this crust, and turn large areas pinkish purple. The color is a pigment that helps them to extract energy from sunlight.

Thermophiles are archaea that can survive in very hot places. For example, there are archaea around many hot springs and geysers. Some of them are only able to grow well at temperatures above 140°C (284°F).

Acidophiles and alkaliphiles live either in very **acid** or very **alkaline** conditions. They survive because they have a kind of pump which shifts the substances that cause the acid or alkaline conditions across the cell membrane. This stops the inside of the microbe from becoming too acid or alkaline.

Thermophiles and laundry detergent

Humans have found several ways of using extreme microbes. Biological washing liquids use proteins from thermophile microbes, which can remove stains even in a hot wash. Mining companies have found that they can use rock-eating microbes to extract valuable metals from waste rock. And methanogens are part of the process by which **biogas** is made from **sewage**.

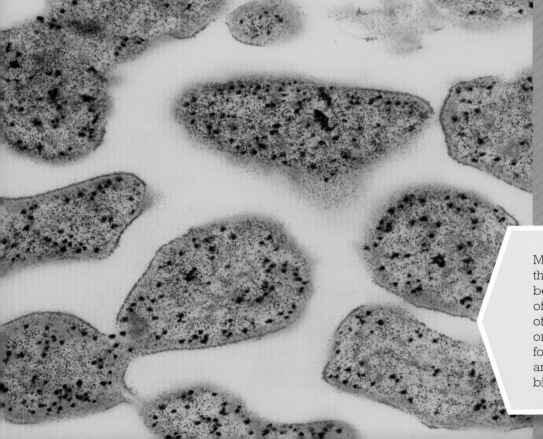

Many scientists think that archaea could be the oldest types of living thing. Traces of archaea-like organisms have been found in rocks that are as much as 3.8 billion years old.

Shifting the goalposts

The conditions under which extremophile microbes can survive have "shifted the goalposts" for life beyond the Earth. Scientists have realized that their ideas about where living things can survive were too narrow. Living things could survive in many places in the solar system.

The surface of Venus today is a hellish place where nothing could survive. But in the past Venus may have been a warm, watery planet. If living things did develop there, then they may have survived in the air. On Earth, some types of bacteria live and reproduce in clouds. The same could possibly happen on Venus. Venusian clouds are found high in the atmosphere, where it is cooler. The clouds are made mainly of sulfuric acid, which would be deadly for most living things. But some acidophiles on Earth can survive in very acid places. Perhaps living things on Venus can, too.

Buried in the ground

On Earth there are extremophiles deep underground as well as in the clouds. This has led scientists to look for underground life elsewhere in the solar system. The environment underground stays at a fairly constant temperature rather than changing with the days and seasons.

The Europa Jupiter System Mission is an ambitious plan to send several space probes to explore Jupiter's moons Europa and Ganymede. The mission would give us many more clues as to whether either of the moons could support life.

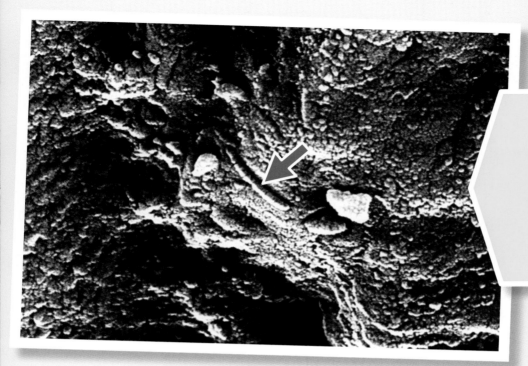

A magnified photo of part of the Mars meteorite ALH 84001. Some scientists think that structures like the one in the center (see arrow) could be fossil microbes.

On Mars, some photos of the surface show openings in the surface and signs of tunnels below ground. Underground caves on Mars could have constant temperatures, and water, or at least ice. Extremophiles found in ice caves in Iceland and Greenland could probably survive perfectly well in these conditions.

The moons Europa, Titan, and Enceladus are other candidates for underground life.

Traveling microbes?

Live bacteria are found very high in the Earth's atmosphere, and they could possibly survive a journey through space as cysts (see page 8). Microbes could have traveled either from other planets to Earth, or from Earth to other parts of the solar system. Perhaps the first living things on Earth were microbes from Mars!

Attack of the Martian bugs!

In 1996 newspapers announced that Martian bugs had arrived on Earth 13,000 years ago. Scientists had found what they thought could be signs of life in a **meteorite** from Mars that landed 13,000 years ago. Later research suggested that the evidence was incorrect, but scientists continue to study the meteorite today.

Most of the extrasolar planets discovered have been gas giants. Some of them are much bigger than even Jupiter.

Life among the stars?

Could there be life beyond the solar system? Our galaxy, the Milky Way, contains over 100 billion stars. Beyond the Milky Way there are billions more galaxies and stars. Could any of these stars have planets that support life?

Until the 1990s, nobody knew if other stars had planets. Then in 1995 astronomers Michel Mayor and Didier Queloz, working in Geneva, Switzerland, detected a planet circling a star known as 51 Pegasi. The planet is a giant gas planet similar to Jupiter. Its official name is 51 Pegasi b, but it is also known as Bellerophon. It orbits very close to the star — far closer than Mercury is to the Sun — and takes only four Earth days for each orbit.

Hundreds of discoveries

Since the discovery of Bellerophon, scientists have found many more planets. The total is now more than 450. They are called extrasolar planets, or **exoplanets**.

Most of the planets found so far have been the size of Jupiter or bigger, because large planets are easier to detect than small ones. So far, only a few rocky planets have been detected and all of them are "super Earths," planets bigger and heavier than Earth. But scientists estimate that lighter planets are actually more common than giant ones. Some stars have several planets. The star Gliese 581, for example, has four planets orbiting it.

Another solar system

In 2010, astronomers using a telescope in Chile discovered a new solar system. The new system has at least five planets, and may have as many as seven. Star HD 10180 is 127 light-years away and is similar in size to our Sun. The five planets found so far are around the size of Neptune. One of the two unconfirmed planets is not much bigger than Earth, but orbits scorchingly close to the star.

Finding planets

Finding a planet orbiting a distant star is not easy. The planet is a tiny speck next to the huge star, which shines between a million and ten billion times more brightly.

When a star has one or more planets orbiting it, the planets affect the way the star spins, giving it a small "wobble." Most planets (including Bellerophon) have been discovered when astronomers detect this wobble.

Another way of finding planets is called the **transit method**. When a planet passes across the face of a star as it orbits, a tiny fraction of its light is blocked and the star dims. When the planet moves around the "back" of the star, the light brightens once again. Some planets have been discovered by measuring these incredibly tiny changes in a star's brightness.

As an exoplanet transits (moves across the face of a star), it cuts off a very tiny part of the star's light. Astronomers are able to detect this drop in brightness.

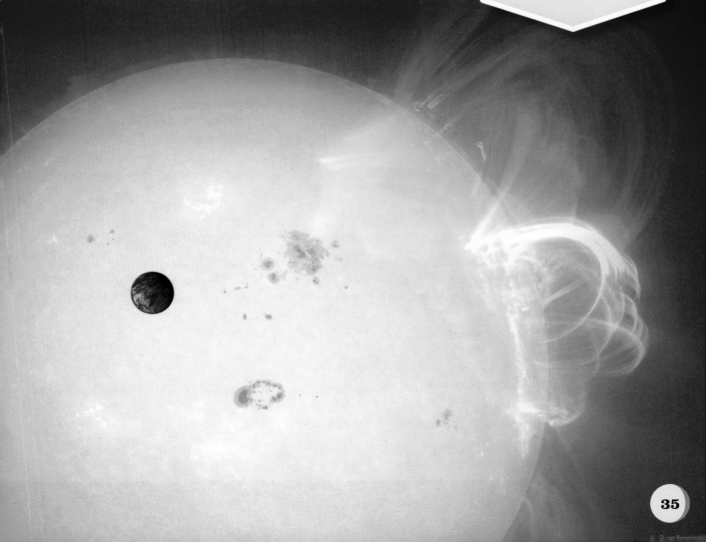

© D. van Ravenswaai

This computer-enhanced picture is one of the first direct images of an exoplanet. On the right is the star, a brown dwarf star called 2M1207. The red dot on the left is the planet.

A space telescope for planet searching

In 2009, the U.S. space agency NASA launched the Kepler Space Telescope with the goal of searching for exoplanets. Kepler is searching about 150,000 stars to find planets in the "local" area of our galaxy. Early results from Kepler found over 1,000 stars that may have planets.

Seeing planets

Planet-finding techniques have greatly improved since Bellerophon was discovered. It is now possible to observe some planets directly. One way of doing this is to block out the main light from the star itself, leaving only the corona (the halo of light around the star). The dim light from any planets can then be seen. Planets show up better in infrared (heat emissons) than in normal light.

The most promising new technique for finding exoplanets is **interferometry**. Several telescopes are used to look at a star from slightly different angles. The different views can be combined to work together as a single giant telescope. Interferometry also makes it possible to cancel out the light from a star, making planets visible.

Searching for life

So far, no really Earth-like planet has been found, but a few have come close. In 2007, a team of scientists in London discovered water vapor in the atmosphere of a large planet called HD 209458 b by analyzing the **spectrum** of light from the planet. However the planet could not support life because it is extremely hot.

In 2010, scientists published new findings about a planet orbiting the star Gliese 581. This planet, Gliese 581g, orbits inside the habitable zone of the star. Scientists also think that it is a rocky planet with enough mass to have an atmosphere. These things tell us that the planet has a good chance of supporting life.

The watery truth

"Distant planet has water!" "Water found on extrasolar planet!" News reporters around the world picked up on the discovery of water vapor on planet HD 209458 b. Travis Barman, one of the team that made the discovery, said "The media sort of went nuts with the story. They let their imaginations run wild, totally wild. I was very careful to say it was water vapor and not liquid water — many did not make that distinction."

An artist's impression of the Gliese 581 planetary system as seen from the surface of Gliese 581d.

Calling all aliens

With so many planets in the Universe, it seems quite possible that intelligent life could have developed on at least one of them. But how will we find it?

Since we have begun exploring space, humans have sent out various messages that could one day be picked up by other intelligent beings. Two space probes launched between 1972 and 1973, Pioneer 10 and Pioneer 11, each had a message engraved on a metal plaque on the side of the spacecraft. It showed pictures of a man and a woman, a star map showing the position of the Sun, and a diagram showing which planet in the solar system we come from. In 1977 two more space probes, Voyager 1 and Voyager 2, carried a videodisc into space, containing images and sounds from the Earth.

The chances of a message on a space probe being picked up are very slim. A more promising way of sending messages is via radio signals. Radio waves travel at the speed of light, and fan out over a wide area as they get further away. Powerful transmitters send out thousands of TV broadcasts, radio programs, and satellite communications each day. Any of these transmissions might be picked up by intelligent beings.

This is the cover of the discs carried by the Voyager 1 and 2 space probes. The diagrams show how to play the disc, how to make the pictures from the recorded information, and the location of Earth in relation to 14 stars called pulsars.

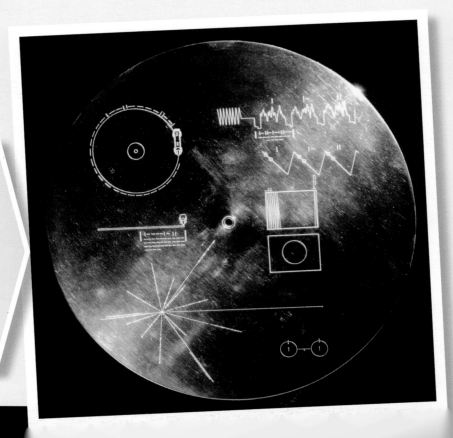

In movies and books, intelligent aliens are usually shown as being similar to humans. In truth, we have no real idea what alien creatures might look like.

Listening for life

Some messages have been sent out with the aim of making contact with intelligent life. However, scientists have concentrated on listening for messages rather than sending them. In 1978, SETI (Search for Extra-Terrestrial Intelligence) began using spare time on radio telescopes to listen for radio signals from space. Later the SETI project expanded and improved and was renamed Sentinel and then META. So far no alien messages have been picked up — but who knows when a transmission might arrive?

Stars, galaxies, and gas clouds in space produce large amounts of radio "noise." However, in one part of the radio spectrum the Universe is generally "quiet," and this is where telescopes listen for radio signals from extraterrestrial life.

An alien visit

People have imagined aliens in all kinds of ways in stories and films. Often, alien invaders arrive from space and threaten to destroy humans altogether. The scientist Stephen Hawking thinks that this is probably what would happen if aliens ever got in contact. "If aliens visit us, it would be much as when Columbus landed in America, which didn't turn out well for the Native Americans."

Conclusion

What are the essentials for life to exist? A hundred years ago, the answer to this question would have been very different from the answer today. Scientists have learned that life can survive in far more harsh conditions than we ever thought possible. In fact, if scientists are right about conditions on the early Earth, life probably began in conditions that would kill most modern animals and plants.

Water bears are tiny creatures found in many environments. They are able to survive freezing and roasting temperatures, and can even stand huge doses of radiation.

Is there life elsewhere in our solar system? A hundred years ago, scientists had virtually no evidence to go on. Today, over fifty years of space exploration has shown that there are no obvious signs of life on any of the main planets and moons. However, we have found some of the essentials for life in surprising places: water underground on Europa and perhaps Mars, organic molecules on Mars and Titan, and an atmosphere on Titan. There are hints that life could still lurk in hidden places. Missions to Mars and Titan are already being planned to check out these hidden places.

Life among the stars

What about life beyond the solar system, on planets circling other stars? Even 30 years ago, scientists had no solid evidence that exoplanets even existed. Today we have detailed information about nearly 500 planets, and strong evidence that there are billions more. Within a few years we may find planets as suitable for life as the Earth.

Are there intelligent aliens out there? This is the most difficult question to answer. Given the huge numbers of planets around other stars, it seems quite possible that there are intelligent aliens somewhere in the Universe. But distances are so vast that contacting another intelligent race could take many years. For example, in 1974 astronomers beamed a powerful radio message out towards a cluster of 300,000 stars. The message was a million times stronger than a TV broadcast. However, it will take 25,000 years to reach the stars it is aimed at. The earliest a message could be sent back would be the year 52,000 CE. By then, perhaps humans will be ready to send out a space mission to meet any aliens who reply.

Do any of these millions of stars support life? Perhaps astronomers will find out within your lifetime. Perhaps you will be the one who finds out!

Timeline of Planet Discoveries

1988 Astronomers observe a "wobble" in the spin of the star Gamma Cephei that suggests it has a planet orbiting it. But, the existence of the planet is not confirmed by other groups of scientists until 2002.

1992 Several planets are observed orbiting a pulsar (a type of dead star).

1995 Michel Mayor and Didier Queloz discover the first extrasolar planet orbiting a "live" star, 51 Pegasi b (Bellerophon).

1996 A massive planet, Tau Bootis b, is discovered by Geoffrey Marcy and Paul Butler of San Francisco University. Marcy went on to become the world's most successful exoplanet hunter: he discovered 70 of the first 100 exoplanets.

1998 The first planet is discovered orbiting the red dwarf star Gliese 876b. More planets were later discovered.

1999 The first star with multiple planets orbiting it is found — Upsilon Andromedae. Three planets are found, all Jupiter-like.

1999 The first planet (HD 209458 b) is found using the transit method.

2002 A planet is discovered orbiting the giant star Iota Draconis (Iota Draconis b). This was the first evidence that planets could survive orbiting giant stars.

2004 The first "super-Earth" is discovered orbiting the star Mu Arae. The planet is about 14 times heavier than Earth.

2005 Two planets, TrES-1 and HD 209458 b, are the first to be observed directly, using the Spitzer Space Telescope.

2006 One of the most distant planets yet found, OGLE-2005-BLG-390Lb, is observed orbiting a red dwarf star 25,000 light-years from Earth.

2007 Scientists are able to analyze the atmosphere of two planets, HD 209458 b and HD 189733 b, for the first time. Water vapor is found in the atmosphere of planet HD 189733 b.

2008 In a follow-up study, the organic molecule methane is found in the atmosphere of planet HD 189733 b.

2008 The first visible light image of an exoplanet, Fomalhaut b, is taken with the Hubble Space Telescope.

2008 Astronomers take the first pictures of a multi-planet solar system, much like ours, orbiting another star. The picture, taken with the Keck and Gemini telescopes, shows three planets orbiting the star HR8799.

2009 The smallest exoplanet yet seen is discovered orbiting the star COROT-7b. The planet is 1.7 times bigger than the Earth.

2009 Gliese 581d, one of four known planets (at the time) orbiting the red dwarf star Gliese 581, is thought to be possibly able to support life, despite not orbiting in the habitable zone of the star.

2009 Measurements suggest that the super-Earth planet GJ 1214 b may be an ocean planet.

2009 The Kepler Space Telescope is launched. It is the first telescope specifically designed for planet hunting.

2010 A "solar system" of seven planets is found orbiting the star HD 10180, 127 light-years from Earth.

2010 Two new planets are discovered orbiting Gliese 581. One of these, Gliese 581g, is the first exoplanet discovered orbiting inside the habitable zone of its star. Scientists think the planet would likely be able to support life.

Names of extrasolar planets

Extrasolar planets are named after the star they orbit. So 51 Pegasi b orbits the star 51 Pegasi.

The star itself is counted as "a," so the first planet to be discovered orbiting a particular star is called "[star name] b."

If more than one planet orbits a star, later discoveries are named c, d, e, etc. So Gliese 581d is the third planet to be discovered orbiting the star Gliese 581.

Exoplanets are named in order of discovery, not in terms of their distance from the star. So Gliese 581e orbits closer to the star than Gliese 581d.

Glossary

acid sour tasting or corrosive substance that can be dissolved in water and turns litmus red

alkali compound that can be dissolved in water and turns litmus blue

atmosphere layer of gases that surrounds a planet

bacteria very small, single-celled organisms whose cells have a very simple structure

biogas gas (mainly methane) and carbon dioxide, formed when microbes ferment plant or animal material

cell basic unit of living things: a small capsule of living material surrounded by a thin outer membrane

cyst tough outer coat that some kinds of bacteria form when they run out of food or find themselves in harsh conditions

DNA genetic material of nearly all living things

dormant in a resting state, maintaining only the minimum processes to sustain life

element simplest type of substance, made up of only one type of atom

exoplanet (extrasolar planet) planet orbiting a star other than the Sun

fossil fuels oil, natural gas, and coal

gravity force that attracts things towards the center of Earth (or another planet, star, or galaxy)

hydrothermal vent hot spring on the seabed deep below the ocean

insulator something that resists the passage of heat or electricity

interferometry technique used to improve the images produced by telescopes, by combining the information from several telescopes

magnetosphere magnetic field around a planet

mass amount of matter an object contains

meteorite rock that falls to Earth from space

methane flammable gas. Natural gas is almost pure methane.

mineral simple chemical including metals and elements such as calcium

molten melted, liquid

photosynthesis process by which plants make food (sugars) from water and carbon dioxide, using energy from sunlight

protein substance that makes up large parts of the structure of living things and controls most of the chemical processes in cells

sewage waste water from houses and offices

silica silicon dioxide, most often found on Earth as quartz rock or as sand

solar system our Sun and its family of planets, asteroids, and all other objects that orbit around it

solar wind a stream of very tiny, electrically charged particles produced by the Sun, which spread outwards across the solar system in a constant wind

spectrum light or other radiation separated into its different colors, or wavelengths

spore tiny seed, like fine powder, produced by a fungus

transit method method of finding exoplanets by detecting tiny variations in the light from a star as a planet passes in front of it

vapor gas phase of water and other liquids

Find Out More

Books

Asimov, Isaac. *Is There Life in Outer Space?* Milwaukee, WI: Gareth Stevens, 2005.

Bortz, Fred. *Cool Science: Astrobiology*. Minneapolis, MN: Lerner, 2008.

Lindop, Laurie. *Science on the Edge: Venturing the Deep Sea*. Minneapolis, MN: Twenty-First Century Books, 2006.

Oxlade, Chris. *The Mystery of Life on Other Planets*. Chicago, IL: Heinemann Library, 2008.

Skurzynski, Gloria. *Are We Alone?: Scientists Search for Life in Space*. Washington, DC: National Geographic Society, 2004.

Winner, Cherie. *Cool Science: Life on the Edge*. Minneapolis, MN: Lerner, 2006.

Websites

http://solarsystem.nasa.gov/kids/index.cfm
Explore the solar system for yourself.

http://serc.carleton.edu/microbelife/extreme/
Learn about extreme microbes and the places they live.

www.ceoe.udel.edu/extreme2004/geology/hydrothermalvents/index.html
Information on hydrothermal vents from the University of Delaware.

www.whoi.edu/page.do?pid=8422
Information on the submersible that was used to discover the first deep-sea hydrothermal vents.

www.pbs.org/wgbh/nova/abyss/life/extremes.html
The story of a trip to the ocean floor to study hydrothermal vents.

http://ngm.nationalgeographic.com/ngm/0308/feature3/
A website about the Atacama Desert.

http://news.nationalgeographic.com/news/2008/05/080522-idaho-mars.html
A short article about the flooding that may have sculpted the surface of Mars billions of years ago.

http://science.nasa.gov/science-news/science-at-nasa/2008/21nov_plasmoids/
NASA news on a study of the effects of the solar wind on Mars.

http://nineplanets.org/europa.html
Information about Europa from the Nine Planets website.

http://astrobiology.nasa.gov/
Astrobiology is the search for life in space. Find out more about life in strange places on Earth, and space missions to search for life beyond the Earth.

http://planetquest.jpl.nasa.gov/index.cfm
JPL website on exoplanet exploration.

http://news.discovery.com/space/travis-barman-keck-exoplanet.html
An interview with Travis Barman, a scientist who searches for new exoplanets.

http://planetquest.jpl.nasa.gov/SIM/Demo/index.cfm
Could you find an exoplanet using an interferometer? This is your chance to try. Complicated but fascinating.

http://planetquest.jpl.nasa.gov/missions/keplerMission.cfm
Information on the first planet-hunting telescope.

Index